PSYCHOPATH

THE PSYCHOPATH LAID BARE

PSYCHOPATHY, RELATIONSHIP FRAUD & MIND GAMES

CAROL FRANKLIN

© 2016

COPYRIGHT NOTICE

DISCLAIMER

Although the author and publisher have made every effort to ensure that the information in this book was correct at press time, the author and publisher do not assume and hereby disclaim any liability to any party for any loss, damage, or disruption caused by errors or omissions, whether such errors or omissions result from negligence, accident, or any other cause.

This book is not intended as a substitute for the medical advice of physicians. The reader should regularly consult a physician in matters relating to his/her health and particularly with respect to any symptoms that may require diagnosis or medical attention.

TABLE OF CONTENTS

INTRODUCTION

Mention the word psychopath and most people will conjure up images of Hannibal Lecture or Jack the Ripper, or some other famous serial killer. The title psychopath instantly conveys a sense of the manic, murderous and certainly criminal. In fact, whilst many serial killers can be classed as psychopaths; there are many psychopaths who are not killers, or even criminals. In fact, the latest research suggests that as many as one person in every hundred is actually a psychopath.

Interestingly, a psychopath is surprisingly difficult to spit, even if you know what you are looking for. They are usually intelligent, forward thinkers but lack an emotional connection to the world around them. A true psychopath will understand that an important event has happened intellectually but will be unable to make an emotional connection to the event. Instead of witnessing someone's pain and attempting to empathize they will be fascinated by the responses and are likely to attempt to mimic them. Achieving this will enable them to appear to respond correctly in any given situation and appear to be 'normal'.

The concept of the psychopath has been around for many years; it was often called 'madness without delirium' or 'moral insanity'. It wasn't until the late nineteenth century that the term psychopath was first used; it was by a German clinician. Unfortunately, the term became a catch phrase for all types of personality disorders and it was not until the late twentieth century that medical professionals started to differentiate between the different types of personality disorders.

One of the most commonly confused personality disorders is that of the sociopath which contains many similar traits to the psychopath. However the key difference in these two types of personality disorders is the way they react to situations. The sociopath is generally nervous and prone to bursts of rage. They are often found to be poorly educated whilst struggling to integrate with society. The psychopath, on the other hand, is always calm and collected; they are very analytical and usually very intelligent. They can be incredibly charming and manipulative, whilst scheming and planning to the smallest detail. They will, however, be unable to make a genuine emotional connection with anyone.

It is generally agreed that the sociopath is a product of society. They are usually people who have been exposed to a very difficult upbringing an extreme trauma. Their reaction has been to retreat within themselves. A sociopath is capable if forming limited emotional connections; these are usually with people they have known for a long time and have learnt to trust. These relationships can be fragile and are usually very volatile.

A psychopath is born with a defect in the brain; this is the part that controls impulse control and emotions. This is not picked up on at birth and is not usually noticeable as they go through their childhood. The reason for this is that as the psychopath learns to control and mimic those around them they may cause discomfort and pain to others but it is usually passed off as a part of growing up.

It is the lack of emotionally connectivity which makes the psychopath a dangerous and powerful force. They have no concern with how their actions affect others although they are happy to use them to achieve their aims. This makes it possible for a psychopath to rise to the top of any business or political circle; they naturally believe they have the right to control others as they are superior. This self belief is what allows them to commit any crime; they have no fear f the consequences and believe they have the right to do as they please.

Research actually suggests that many top business leaders and politicians are psychopaths; they have the desire and rive to achieve their goals without regard to who is hurt on the way and what others think of them. These qualities can actually assist them in getting to the top of their chosen field! In fact, it is believed that the actual number of psychopaths in top business positions is between three and twenty five percent; much higher than the average one percent of the population.

This figure is hard to confirm as most psychopaths are not aware that they are a psychopath. In fact, they are not aware that there is anything wrong with them.

This book is designed to help you to understand what a psychopath is and how it differs from a sociopath. It provides a basic guideline to the different types of personality disorders, knowledge of these will assist you in understanding whether you are dealing with a psychopath or not. Most importantly the book will highlight the main characteristics of a psychopath and highlight how to spot one.

This is an important skill to develop as you may need to have a relationship with a psychopath through work or a common friend. You may even find that you are living with a psychopath! The book highlights how the psychopath generally operates within relationships and the best approach for dealing with a psychopath. Remember, they are not all criminals, their high intelligence and charm can be beguiling and they can also make a valuable contribution to society.

This book covers the common misconceptions associated with psychopaths and how the disorder is diagnosed along with the prospects for the future; both for the psychopath and the people in their life. What is not possible to establish is what will drive a psychopath to switch from staying within the law to committing a serious crime. If it was possible to understand the motives behind such a switch it would be much easier to diagnose the psychopaths who are at most risk of hurting others. The book will take a look at what criteria and actions can affect their behaviour to see if there is a common trait which can be associated with the start of a psychopath's criminal behaviour.

The more you understand about the psychopath the easier it will be to deal with one when you meet one.

With the estimated number of psychopaths being one in one hundred, it is likely that you have already met at least one!

CHAPTER 1 – PERSONALITY DISORDERS

Your personality is an intrinsic part of who you are; it controls your reactions to certain stimuli both physically and emotionally. It is believed that your personality is a result of your genes and the experiences you have had whilst growing up. A normal personality is one that falls within the average range of emotional responses in any given situation. People who display traits at the extreme end of the scale are defined as having a personality disorder.

The first instance of a personality study was completed by Hippocrates; the original premise was that there were four basic temperaments. All subsequent research has been built upon his initial observations. In modern times the personality is broken down into five distinct categories:

- Openness to new experiences

- Conscience

- Extroversion

- Agreeableness

- Neuroticism

It is believed that the range of reaction in each of these categories will remain static over time; this is a result of the unique gene make up of every human. Differences between two people brought up in the same family in exactly the same way are a direct result of this gene difference. It is also believed that life experience will alter the responses in these categories but only by a small amount. They are not enough, by themselves, to completely change a personality.

There has been an abundance of research into personality development and at what point a personality is established and unlikely to change. This research has also looked at the likelihood of childhood behaviour reflecting future personality traits. It is believed that the personality does not actually stabilize until someone reaches the age of thirty. The temperament displayed as a child is seen as a precursor to the adult personality. By studying children it is possible to predict who will is likely to have a personality disorder and who will not.

It is possible to take a personality test online and establish which type of personality you have. However, these tests may provide a skewed set of results if you do not answer the questions completely honestly; and this can be difficult to do!

To fully understand a personality disorder it is essential to understand how a personality is studied. There are two key areas; personality characteristics and how all the elements of a personality combine.

Personality characteristics covers the ability to integrate socially with others and how irritable or emotion affects the way someone behaves.

The elements of a personality covers all the different emotional and physical reactions to everyday situations. The reaction to a specific incident will be in relation to the levels of each personality trait and it is the study of how small changes in the personality can have a huge effect on the way someone views life and deals with everyday situations. In fact, the human personality is so complicated that a lifetime of study is unlikely to allow you to see all the different variations!

Psychopathy is just one type of personality disorder; the medical profession recognizes ten different disorders which fall into three broad categories. All personality disorders will display following trends:

- An irregular or distorted thinking pattern to what is considered average or normal.

- Emotional difficulties; this can range from an overly emotional response to no emotion at all.

- Poor impulse control, people with personality disorders can have no impulse control and will do anything they want at any time without consideration for others. Alternatively, they may be unable or unwilling to react at all to anything and keep an extremely tight control on their impulses and emotions.

- Difficulty establishing relationships on a deep and meaningful level with any other person.

There are a variety of reasons as to why this can be the case and it is possible that many people with personality disorders can form basic relationships with others.

These categories which all personality disorders fall into are known as clusters:

1. Cluster A

Disorders in this category have what is seen as an odd or eccentric disorder. People who fall into this category will have a personality disorder which makes them socially withdrawn; they will usually feel visibly awkward in a social situation. Sufferers will usually have a pattern of distorted thinking which will make them appear eccentric. Common personality disorders which fall into this category include paranoid personality disorder, schizoid personality disorder and schizotypal personality disorders.

2. Cluster B

This group of disorders are known to create people with highly dramatic tendencies. They will also, usually, be emotional and erratic. As with cluster A, people with a disorder in this cluster will have poor impulse control and they will struggle to control their emotional responses; which can be extreme. Common disorders within this cluster are Borderline Personality Disorder, Narcissistic Personality disorder, Histrionic personality disorder and antisocial personality disorder.

3. Cluster C

Disorders which fall under this category are recognized as belonging to people with fearful and anxious traits. Disorders in this category will often feel unworthy and uncomfortable in social settings. This cluster includes the avoidant personality disorder, dependent personality disorder and obsessive compulsive personality disorders.

Common symptoms of those with a cluster C disorder include isolation; this is a result of a need for order in their life, for everything to be controlled and an obsession about certain things. They are also likely to display a passive aggressive attitude; this will include a self chosen failure, masochistic.

The psychopath is categorised under cluster B and is seen as a type of antisocial personality disorder. The change of name has arisen to help prevent the stereotyping that has becoming common when people think of a psychopath; after all, as already mentioned the first response to the mention of a psychopath is an image of a serial killer.

Interestingly the term psychopath was initially used to describe someone with an outgoing personality and psychotic tendencies. This became a term which covered a wide range of personality disorders as medical professionals started to acknowledge that a psychopath does not need to be a criminal. More recently the medical profession have attempted to clarify the situation by calling all types of these disorders antisocial personality. The term sociopath has even been adopted to help differentiate between those who have psychotic tendencies and those who do not.

In reality this has led to a great deal of confusion about whom and what really classes as a psychopath; this is made more complicated by the lack of concrete evidence and ability to delve into the personality, thoughts and mindset of a true psychopath. There are conflicting opinions even within the medical profession and a general reluctance to use the term psychopath as it is believed this will create a negative image and reaction from those who have been diagnosed and from their friends and relatives.

The psychopath will have four main traits; these are known as:

- antisocial traits

These traits are those which, when reviewed can be seen to be present throughout the childhood years as behaviour issues, which are often missed as they are assumed to simply be a phase of growing up. This behaviour will be visible through the teenage years and often end up in the display if criminal behaviour.

- interpersonal traits

A psychopath will have an inflated notion of their own self importance, it will also become apparent that they are extremely good at manipulating others and will deceive others without a second thought. Their personal traits will also show as an ability to appear socially appealing and even desirable. Upon deeper examination it will be obvious that the psychopath is a habitual liar.

- affective traits

These types of traits include a callous nature and disregard for other people, unless they are useful in achieving a specific goal. Even if this is the case they will be seen as little more than a means to an end. Other people are simply objects. The psychopath will also have a limited ability to provide a genuine emotional response; there will also be a lack of guilt concerning their actions.

- lifestyle traits

The psychopath will often be impulsive and pursue an adrenaline rush in all areas of their live. It is this which helps to drive them to become successful in their chosen activity. In fact, they will usually have an unrealistic expectation for life; this and drive them to try extremely hard to achieve what they believe is possible. But, should they be unable to achieve their goal, for any reason they will find it difficult to deal with the concept that they have a limit. This can lead to a spiral of depression and even more radical behaviour than normal.

A personality disorder will usually be present from birth although it can also be a result of a trauma, such as a car accident, which can cause brain damage. In fact, for a personality disorder to be diagnosed it is essential to be able to see the traits of the disorder as having been present for many years. If this cannot be shown then it is likely that you are simply experiencing a temporary depression or change of personality as a result of a specific incident.

Dealing with a personality disorder in someone you love, such as a partner or family member can be a difficult and challenging pastime. People with personality disorders are frequently unaware that they have a personality disorder. Indeed, if they have had the traits since birth they have no reason to suspect that there is anything wrong with their behaviour.

A personality disorder will usually have a visible effect on someone's life. They may be unable to connect with others in a normal way or lack the ability to process normal responses to certain behaviour. They may even be unable to comprehend the importance of social boundaries and are likely to react in an inappropriate, if not embarrassing way. The very nature of a personality means that you should be able to relate to some of the traits contained in a personality disorder but you will not have the extreme version of many traits.

It is possible to display several traits of a personality disorder and not actually have a personality disorder. The main criteria for confirming the existence of a disorder is that it has a detrimental effect on their daily life. In fact, most people with a personality disorder are only diagnosed as having one when they visit a doctor with symptoms of stress or depression as they are struggling to cope with life.

It is extremely important to note that your personality is part of who you are, it develops and grows as you do and cannot be fixed by taking a pill, or any simple procedure. Research confirms that all treatments need to create an opportunity for people with a disorder to learn to live with it and slowly adapt to a new way of living.

Perhaps the most important thing to understand when dealing with someone with a personality disorder is that this is not a choice; the disorder was present at birth and has grown with them, the way they behave and react now is a result of years of experience behaving the same way. Losing your patience or even giving up is not an option! Just as with any other disease, someone with a personality disorder needs the care and support of their loved ones to help them become better people and live a full and happy life. Even a psychopath can learn the correct response to a given scenario, although they may never feel the expected emotional response. Of course, they will need to choose to follow the right path and, particularly in the case of a psychopath, this can be a difficult process as their inner conscience is telling them they have the right and power to do whatever they want.

No matter whether you are dealing with a loved one or a work colleague, understanding the basic make-up of a personality and both how and why a disorder can arise will help you to deal with them in the best possible way.

Chapter 2 – Common Traits Of A Psychopath & How To Recognize One

A true psychopath will never even consider it a possibility that they have a mental illness. It is possible that if you point out the issue they will investigate the disorder and recognize the symptoms of a psychopath as matching their own behaviour and thought patterns. However, even if they do this they will not see themselves as having a disorder; instead they will study the information with a detached interest and use the knowledge to assist themselves in achieving their aims.

Common traits that all psychopaths will display are:

- High Level of Self Belief

A psychopath believes that they can do anything; they have complete confidence in their ability to achieve a goal, no matter how impossible it may seem to anyone else. This unshakeable belief is often a result of having achieved the impossible in the past; a situation that arises as they have no fear of taking risks or concerns regarding the consequences of any given action.

- No sense of guilt or remorse

A true psychopath has no emotional empathy. They can learn to display the right emotion when required but this is not backed up by a genuine feeling. Being unable to feel the consequences of their actions means that they will attempt anything, regardless of who gets hurt along the way. A lack of emotional empathy also means that they are simply unable to comprehend the affect their actions have on others. If they cannot comprehend the effect on an emotional level then they will be unable to experience any remorse or guilt for their actions. They simply cannot see the error of their actions.

- Deceitful

It is common for a psychopath to lie compulsively. It may be to shift blame and point the finger at someone else. This is a common trick as they usually feel they are above reproach. It may also be to manipulate someone and ensure they complete the task that they have been assigned. As they do not feel guilt or remorse they see no issue with lying as long as it helps them to achieve their desires.

- Irritable

Should you manage to confront a psychopath with the proof that they were wrong and they are unable to blame someone else, they are likely to react with extreme irritability and aggression. They do not like to be questioned or second guessed and will react badly. They may even indulge in some extreme behaviour on order to change the subject and remind everyone just how amazing they are.

- Calm and cool

The majority of the time a psychopath will remain calm, even a show of anger could be simply to manipulate a person to do their bidding. They are generally cold and calculating, considering their options and each move before they do anything. The lack of emotion means that many decisions are black and white, easily made and logical. These decisions may affect others adversely but they will remain focused on their goal. This approach has been successfully adopted by many business people and political leaders. In fact, it is believed that a high percentage of politicians and business people are actually psychopath; effectively hiding in plain sight.

- No concern for safety

A psychopath has no regard for the consequences of an action, other than to propel their own dreams forward. This means that they will undertake many actions which are potentially extremely dangerous; the outcome does not worry them as they believe in themselves and a successful outcome. Many psychopaths are actually incapable of considering that a specific idea will not work.

Safety issues are seen to have a low priority, if they are seen at all. The world is very black and white to a psychopath and even a safety issue can be reduced to will it happen or not. A simple question gets a simple answer and the risk is taken, without being fully assessed.

- Charming

Most, if not all psychopaths are extremely charming. They love to be worshipped and enjoy being the centre of attention at any type of gathering. In fact, to be publically acknowledged gives the; a real buzz. Being able to charm people allows them to manipulate others into doing their bidding; often without the third party being aware that they have been manipulated!

Their charm extends to almost every occasion as they are constantly evaluating and studying a given situation and how best to make any scenario serve their own purpose.

The more a psychopath studies others the easier they will find it to control them; mimic them and even use this information to manipulate others. To them the whole world is a chess board and they are free to move any piece how they see fit.

- Lack of Morals

A psychopath will not have any moral conscience to guide them, they may learn to understand the moral compass that exists in most people's lives but it is not something they will become familiar with. A lack of morals makes it possible to try anything and will make it difficult to have a consistent reaction to any given situation.

- Low Arousal rate

A true psychopath will not experience a rush of excitement or fear when a new incident occurs or a terrible accident happens. Their heart rate will not race; in fact they will not even be able to connect on an emotional level. They will be aware that something important has happened and will study the actions and reactions of the onlookers. This is all useful information to file away for later use.

In fact, the psychopath loves to learn new things, particularly if they can be beneficial to them in the future. If a psychopath becomes violent it is highly likely that their heart rate will actually decrease, despite the physical effort involved in such an attack. It is this lack of arousal, in any situation, which leads to the chilling traditional image of a psychopath.

It may seem surprising but the psychopath does not actually need to be the centre of attention. The way they behave and the fact that they appear very charming often leads to them becoming the life of any party. But, they will simply be playing a part, studying people and manipulating them by appearing to be normal. The true psychopath will be very difficult to spot as they can blend into a group and live, what appears to be, a normal life. Fortunately, there are several ways of spotting a psychopath, even the well hidden ones:

- Street Smart

A psychopath will appear to be tough and knowledgeable of the ways of the world. They will always know what to do and will appear decisive, full of action and experience; it is easy to be led by them in an unfamiliar situation as they appear to be in control. At the same time they will emit an air of goodness and innocence which will make you trust them.

- Contradictory

It is highly likely that the psychopath will contradict themselves. This is not an instant thing; one opinion mentioned this week may be contradicted next week, or even a month or two later. This is not a case of an opinion shift, instead it is simply the fact that the psychopath sees most things in a two dimensional way and their opinion changes according to the factors around them and their own needs. In fact, it can be this contradictory nature that draws you to a psychopath; even if you do not understand why you are being drawn to them.

- Superiority

It will become evident that they feel superior to everyone else around them. They simply believe they are better, their ideas are better and that everyone should do things their way. At times they may appear to be haughty, or arrogant, conversely, you are likely to see these times as out of character when they are, in fact, the true personality of a psychopath showing through.

They may also appear to be amused by your efforts although indifferent to the outcome.

- Story Time

A psychopath loves to tell stories, preferably when everyone stops what they are doing to listen. This feeds their need to be the centre of attention. Their stories will be wild and exciting, bold and brash, as well as bordering on the criminal. The stories will be told in such a way that it appears to be something they have done but would not dream of doing now; they are so much more mature.

It gives the impression of someone who has lived well, possibly gone off the rails slightly, but is now an upstanding pillar of the community.

- Sleep

The genetic make-up of a psychopath means that they will need very little sleep; just four or five hours a night is enough for them to function normally. It is a good thing that their bodies have little need for sleep as they will use this time to find new exciting and stimulating activities.

- They get it wrong!

Psychopaths are accomplished actors, they can role play all day and stimulate the right response to almost any scenario. However, as they are simply using past experience and knowledge to decide on an appropriate response, they sometimes do get it wrong. It will be noticeable that their reaction seems fake, or that there is no response at all.

- Switching emotions

It is possible for a psychopath to appear to be in a state of rage for one minute and then completely calm again a moment later. This is because they do not have the capacity to truly feel any emotion. Rage is the closest they will get but this is usually short lived as they will want to return to their charade and keep you convinced of how nice and normal they are.

- Contempt

A psychopath is, by their very nature, contemptuous of other humans. Others are seen as inferior and possibly even beneath consideration. In their mind they are only listening to you to appear normal whilst they plan their next move. Of course it can be very difficult to see contempt but many psychopaths appear to have a flash of contempt, visible only in their faces for a few milliseconds. They are easily missed!

- Sexual desires

A psychopath will generally have deviant sexual desires; this by itself is not an issue and other people with a variety of deviant desires will be normal and not psychopaths. However, the psychopath will be particularly pushy to get you to indulge in these desires. This is a direct result of not having good impulse control; a psychopath is unlikely to wait or spend an excessive amount of time convincing someone to indulge in their fantasies. It is likely that they will simply take aggressive action to make the fantasy happen.

- Smell

It is believed there is a connection between the sense of smell and the ability to control impulses. The consequence of this is that the majority of psychopaths will have an inability to either smell something or differentiate between smells.

- Ummmm

A psychopath will say 'ummm' and 'aah' a lot. This has been noted by studying known psychopaths and comparing the results to the general population. The reason for saving these phrases often is not known although experts think it may be to allow the psychopath to collect their thoughts and make sure they are creating the right impression.

- Emotions

It is simply not possible for a psychopath to tell you a story about the time they genuinely experienced an emotion. This information will not be obvious as they are experts at blending in and appearing normal, however, if you push them you will find that this principle is true. Their only knowledge of emotions is what they have learned by watching and copying others.

- Startling

A psychopath will not startle easily as they have no real emotions or concept of fear. They will not attempt to mask this attribute as they do not realise its important, this means you must question the type of person you are with if they do not react when a car back-fires, or some other loud noise happens behind you.

- Personal Space

Everyone likes to have their own personal space; it is both intimidating and annoying when someone keeps pushing themselves into your personal space. A psychopath does not have the same feeling regarding personal space and does not understand your need for it. Research has actually shown that repeatedly entering your space is similar to how predators act before they go for the kill. The psychopath is the predator and you are in danger of becoming their prey! Invading your personal space is also an aggressive way of signalling their power over you and ability to manipulate you.

- Hints

One way in which a psychopath will play with your emotions, although you are unlikely to realise it at the time, is to tell you they are not good for you. They may inform you that you are too trusting and that this quality will make you an easy target for any con artist. The comment will appear to be said in a concerned, friendly way when in fact it is them that will abuse your trust.

It is incredibly difficult to spot an isolated incident such as this, but, as time passes there will be repeated occasions when this happens and you will gradually be able to spot the pattern, or at the least, the fact that it keeps happening and that it is not, actually your fault.

Why?

You may wish to know why a psychopath would go to such extremes in order just to manipulate you, aside from the obvious motivation of reaching their desired destination. The derive pleasure, even a buzz of excitement every time they are successful in duping someone; they will experience pleasure that they are able to control someone else. Of course, the more times they successfully dupe you the more likely it is that you will realise and they will be exposed. This is why psychopaths generally dupe people towards the end of a relationship; when they are ready to move onto new pastures.

It is important to note that no matter how much you study people and become aware of your surroundings, a true psychopath will be able to blend it and take advantage of your good nature without you realising it. Even professionals can be duped by a psychopath as they mimic the right behaviour.

CHAPTER 3 – COMMON MISCONCEPTIONS

The psychopath has often been mentioned on the news and medical research programs, it is this ease of use that has lead to the stereotypical image of a psychopath and too many common misconceptions about the psychopathic personality.

- Bloodthirsty

As already mentioned the average psychopath is not a serial killer. However, this is the impression that is created by the news, the reason for this is that the most prolific serial killers, such as Ted Bundy, or fictitious characters such as Hannibal Lecture are seen to be psychopaths. As most people do not come across the term, 'psychopath', in their everyday lives a connection is made between a psychopath and the criminally insane.

Of course, the reality is more difficult to appreciate; the thought that any person you meet could be a psychopath could lead to a paranoid personality disorder!

- Rarity

You could be forgiven for thinking that the number of psychopaths in the world is limited; those that are, live outside the law and are handled as and when they need to be. This is, again, tied in with the image you are presented with by the media. Seeing a psychopath as a cold blooded killer means you do not recognize the fact that they can be hiding in plain sight, manipulating and manoeuvring all the time to ensure they get where they want to go.

As an estimated one percent of the population are psychopaths there are literally millions of them around the world; perhaps it is tile to ask yourself if you are one?

- Insanity

It is easy and perhaps preferable to imagine that all psychopaths are insane; certainly the common view of them would back up this statement. However, the American Psychiatric Association and many other medical bodies confirm that a psychopath is not insane; they are capable of understanding right and wrong. The fact that they then choose to follow their own path, regardless of whether the general public consider it to be wrong, is simply a reflection of their belief that they are superior and can do whatever they like. There is no proof that a psychopath experiences hallucinations or voices in their head.

- Mass Murderers are psychopaths

Whilst it is true that some serial killers are psychopaths, the more carefully they plan the event the more likely they are to fit into this category. However, the majority if mass murderers are labelled as psychopaths when they are actually psychotic; which is a mental illness.

- Prisons are full of Psychopaths

Whilst this might make it easier to understand and tolerate those who are inside a prison it is simply not true. It is estimated that between twenty and twenty five percent of the prison population are psychopaths. The rest are, almost by default, suffering with antisocial personality disorders. The reason this is by default is that the majority of people in prison are there as they have committed a deed which is seen to be outside of the acceptable behaviour by society. This description over lacks with that of the antisocial personality; someone who acts and behaves in an antisocial way! It could be said that the disorder was created to cover the prison population as it is a very general term.

- There is no cure for Psychopathy

Treatment options and future prospects are discussed in detail later in this book. However, it is worth noting that the long established view has been that there is no cure or treatment method which will work on a psychopath. Thankfully, very recent studies and trials have shown that there are possibilities concerning the treatment of this disorder. With skilled, specialist care it is possible to change the behaviour of even the most committed psychopath.

- It is a recognized Medical disorder

It is interesting that antisocial personality disorder is recognized by a variety of medical bodies and yet psychopathy is not. Although it is often incorporated within the description of antisocial personality disorders there are key differences. Whilst the antisocial personality disorder can be diagnosed through tests and establishing that someone displays all the relevant traits to qualify. The psychopath is much harder to diagnose as they may not display all the traits associated with psychopathy. This is not because they do not have the traits but is because they have managed to keep these traits hidden.

It is believed that the term psychopath became known by the general public as it was a term which could be used to explain people who committed heinous acts. At the end of the twentieth century the concept of psychopathy graduated from a plausible but vague theory into a legitimate disorder and all forms of media have pushed this image since. However, despite this, medical boards across the world have not yet recognized the disorder in its own right.

- Planning

A psychopath is capable of planning and executing a plan to the most minute detail; it is this skill, combined with the appearance of being 'normal' that allows a psychopath to manipulate and manoeuvre others to achieve their own goals. However, not every criminal or manipulative act is a result of this extensive planning. Psychopaths generally have poor impulse control which means they can react extremely badly to the simplest of things; such as a challenge to their authority. Acts conducted while they are operating under impulse have no methodical planning and are the most likely way of exposing a psychopath.

- They cannot learn from their mistakes

In effect this is true. A psychopath does not care about whether something is right or wrong and what the consequences of an action are. They will happily repeat an action if they believe it will benefit them again. However, they are capable of learning from their mistakes.

Most psychopaths are intelligent and understand right and wrong. They will be able to assess and understand what was wrong with their behaviour, even if they do not emotionally connect or fear the consequences. However, they are intelligent enough to understand the importance of either dealing with something differently next time or adapting their technique. This is a way of learning from their mistakes, even if the motivation behind this is to ensure they avoid detection or difficult explanations in the future.

- Top Business leaders and Politicians are psychopaths

This is a common misconception as the most successful people often display psychopathic traits. This is because to be successful in business or politics takes an ability to ignore the comments of others and focus on your own goal. Leaders can appear to be callous and superior to others; all traits of a psychopath. However, many of these business leaders and politicians are simply dedicated to being the best they can be; they know that the only way to truly succeed is to believe in themselves and keep going, regardless of the consequences.

Having some of the traits that are commonly found in a psychopath does not make them a psychopath! To be called a psychopath you must display the majority, if not all of the traits described in this book; you must also be devoid of emotional responses. Most business leaders and politicians actually care deeply for others and are emotionally connected to their cause.

It is, however, true that as many as four percent of business leaders and politicians do have all the symptoms of a psychopath and can be classed as one. This is four times the average that is seen in the general population and maybe enough to make you think twice! There are theories that connect the high presence of psychopaths and their carefree nature with the economic recession and global crisis of recent years. It may be better to consider if the number of psychopaths is on the increase, and if so, what that says for the future of the world!

- The description of a psychopath is adhered to by all medical professionals

When a disorder is recognized it is normal to create a list of symptoms, treatment options and even how to detect the disorder. It can then be assessed and registered with the relevant professional bodies. However, this is not the case with the psychopath.

Medical professionals do agree that criminals who are classed as psychopaths will be callous, emotional distant, aggressive and have no trace of guilt or remorse. However, once the concept is transferred into the general, non criminal, society there are substantial differences in how medical professionals categorize and diagnose a psychopath.

It is possible for a psychopath to be cold-hearted, callous, lacking in empathy and to have a very shallow emotional base. It is also possible to call someone a psychopath when they are cold-hearted, callous, lacking in empathy and anxious. The two conditions have a significant difference in the way they interact with others but have the same lack of empathy and ability to act without feeling. The question which has been raised is whether the psychopath should be sub-divided into successful or not, or a variety of other criteria to decide whether a psychopath is likely to be problematic or not to the rest of society. It is clear there are still many issues surrounding the diagnosis of a psychopath.

Chapter 4 – Relationship Fraud, Mind Games & Living With A Psychopath

The psychopath is happy to adapt the truth to fit their needs and desires; if part of this adaption is committing to a relationship in order to present the right image or help them achieve their goals they will happily do so. As consummate actors they will happily act the part of a good partner, they may even give you flowers and other treats to ensure you are happy; and doing what they need you to. It is important to remember that, if you are in a relationship with a psychopath they will be constantly manipulating you and evaluating you to ensure they get what they want or need. They are so good at this that it is highly unlikely that you will even realise what they are doing.

It is only when you start to notice the small irregularities that you will question their personality and their love, research on the internet will probably help you to realise that they are potentially a psychopath and not good for you. However, it can be difficult to end a relationship with a psychopath as they enjoy the control they have over you; they will usually convince you to stay until they are ready to end it. It is also often exceptionally difficult to finish a relationship as the fear of the future can make it seem easier to stay where you are.

The hardest part is realising that the relationship you have put your heart and soul into means nothing to your partner; it was a means to an end, not an end in itself. In essence the relationship was no more than a mind game to the psychopath. They dominated you with the power of their mind and used this power to keep you doing their bidding as and when required.

There are two main types of relationship fraud:

Love

The obvious casualty is love. You fall in love with someone and attempt to do whatever it takes to make them happy, in return you get a fake love which allows them to infiltrate your life, learn you strengths and weaknesses and exploit them for their own benefit.

Financial

Relationship fraud can simply be completed in order to access your money or borrow money in your name. The psychopath will access as much money as they possibly can in your name and then disappear without worrying about the consequences and the mess you are left with.

There are a variety of behaviour issues which can give away the fact that you are living with or dating a psychopath, it is important to be aware of them; this will ensure you can act or react to minimize any issues and prevent the opportunity for relationship fraud:

- Bragging

A common trait of any psychopath is the need to brag about their achievements, many of these will be impossible to prove or disapprove. If it is possible to check you will probably find that the details have been exaggerated to make the psychopath look better; quite possibly at the expense of others. Bragging allows them to be the centre of attention and to feel important; something that a psychopath believes they have the right to.

If you meet someone who brags a lot approach with caution!

- Cruelty

Psychopaths have no real emotion and will not react to cruelty with horror. They will either react in a distracted, distant way; simply studying the effects and reactions of all parties involved, or they will find the cruelty amusing. This is a reflection of their character; other people and animals are simply an entertaining distraction to them. They may even laugh at someone else's pain, if you witness this escape while you can!

- Knowledge

Despite their grandiose bragging you will eventually realise that they know a lot more about you than you do about them. This is because they do not like giving away personal information and will spend their time discovering all they can about you. This will make it seem as though they are interested in you and the things you like to do, when, in fact, they are building a profile of your strengths and weaknesses. This will allow them to control and manipulate you. It may be advisable to look at what you know about a new partner and if it is not much you may want to verify some or all of the information you have.

- Narrowing Tactics

A psychopath will work towards separating you from your family and friends; this will ensure you are reliant on them and more receptive to their ideas and plans. The process of separating you will be done slowly and through a variety of carefully timed phrases and conjectures. The more separated you become the harder it will be for you to see that the psychopath in your life is not good for you. This is their aim and can be easy to achieve as many of the things they do can be construed as signs of love and affection.

- Borrowing Money

Many psychopaths are successful and have access to plenty of funds. However, they do not like spending them as they feel that they are entitled to anything they want and that extends to others paying for things for them. Forgetting their wallet once is acceptable, a second time should get you asking questions.

Learning about you and feigning interest is only the first step, to ensure the psychopath has long term control over you and gains the power and advantage they seek, they need to play mind games. The best way to defend against these is to understand how they deceive and manipulate:

- Metaphors

As mentioned, much of what the average psychopath says is fabricated, they weave a web of lies which surrounds them and will encompass you, if you allow it. In order to ensure you follow the path they want you to they will use an analogy or metaphor to illustrate a point. When used correctly it will make sense and sound like a good reason to cheat on your partner or run someone over. In fact, it will sound like the right thing to do! However, if you pick the analogy apart you will see it is not the right path to follow.

- Slander

Rather than accept that their plan may have gone awry they will blame anyone and everyone else, including their partner. This approach can also be used to confirm their credibility.

- Avoidance

If you ask a psychopath a direct question they will smoothly change the subject and flatter you or talk about something different. Their idea is to ensure you forget your question and the conversation moves on somewhere else. Alternatively, instead of a specific answer they will talk about humanity and general issues which loosely relate to the original question.

- Details

The more detail a psychopath provides the more convincing the lie is. This is because it is difficult to fabricate such a complex story. However, it is even more difficult to maintain a story such as this and the psychopath can often be caught out by asking them a similar question to gauge their response a week or two later.

- Emotional Play

The psychopath is an excellent manipulator of emotions and will use them to ensure you forget your query and believe what they are saying. For example, when confronted by two people with different versions of the same event they will use emotional blackmail to ensure you side with them. Your feelings for the psychopath will ensure that you quickly agree with their version and side with them. To anyone outside the events it will be obvious you are being manipulated, but it will not be to you.

Despite heeding the warnings and learning about psychopaths it remains a possibility that you will fall under their spell and fall in love with a psychopath. If this does happen then it is essential to understand the best ways to live with one and how to make the relationship work for you. Alternatively, you can simply pluck up the courage to leave them.

- Accept it

The most important thing you can do is accept the fact that your partner is a psychopath. As already mentioned this does not automatically make them a criminal. It does mean they will be used to manipulating people and getting their own way. Accepting that they are a psychopath will allow you to take steps to deal with them, you will also need to evaluate your relationship and see if it is worth saving. It is possible to live with a psychopath providing you are aware of their true nature and know how to deal with them.

- Leave them

The best course of action can be to simply walk away, you will not be at risk of being manipulated or hurt by the psychopath then! However, this is much easier said than done, particularly if you have children together, have been together for a long time or the person is a relative. In these instances you will need to stick to the following guidelines.

- Self-analysis

Having accepted the situation you also need to accept that the psychopath latched onto you for a reason. Understanding what this reason is will help you to either prevent them from manipulating you in the future or may even give you the opportunity to manipulate them and get them help. They may have been drawn to you by your creative nature or your ability to love so easily; these are qualities they may crave in themselves and being with you will help them to learn to mimic them. Alternatively they may have seen you as an easy target; someone who they will be able to manipulate easily. A psychopath is likely to be drawn to someone who displays characteristics they do not possess. The easiest way of assessing why they choose you may be to think about how they have changed since you have been together.

- Don't Reason

The psychopath likes to be right, attempting to reason with them is likely to anger them and get you nowhere. Instead think the problem through and present them with the solution you are prepared to accept. At this point you should leave them to it, change the subject or go out. It is essential for them to realise that you are not going to change your mind, you have made your decision and they will need to accept it. The shift in power may go against their grain but they may be prepared to accept it in order to gain the other benefits they already have, or could have.

- Remain Cool

It is essential to remain cool, if you feel your temper rising change the subject or leave the room, telling your partner the discussion is over. This will ensure they do not locate another way to get you to react and manipulate you accordingly. The relationship you already have with your psychopathic partner can continue and may be worthwhile if you have been together for a long time and there are no signs of criminal intent. The key to moving the relationship forward and building an even stronger one in the future is to be strong. Build yourself a good support group who can help you know that you are doing the right thing. It is not essential to never give in to the psychopath's demands, it is essential to stand firm when you have made a decision. Never give them the opportunity to manipulate you by using their charm and easy way with words. State your case and leave them to it; they will soon learn when you mean business and when they can still manipulate you.

There is, obviously, a risk to this tactic. The psychopath may decide it is time to move on and find a new person to control. However, this is a risk that must be taken; either you will build a stronger relationship or you will be better off without them. Living with a psychopath is not an easy option, but you may be one of the many people who can't give up until you have tried everything.

CHAPTER 5 - DIAGNOSIS, TREATMENT OPTIONS & FUTURE PROSPECTS

Any personality disorder must be diagnosed by a professional, although it is often not something a professional is keen to do! The reason for this is twofold; firstly, a diagnosis means a possible negative reaction from others who do not fully understand the disorder and this can make it very difficult to treat or support sufferers. This can be particularly true in the case of the psychopath as the mention of the disorder almost always leads to thoughts of serial kills and mass murderers.

The second reason is that many of the personality disorders have similar traits and a few key differences. It is possible to diagnose the wrong disorder and be treating the patient in entirely the wrong way.

It is also very uncommon for a psychopath to seek treatment themselves; they are not likely to think they have an issue as they do not see anything wrong with themselves. The most likely reason a psychopath would be in a doctor's surgery would be if they had an issue with depression or self image and needed confirmation that they were okay. It would not be obvious that they were a psychopath.

If a doctor does suspect someone could be a psychopath then they will ask them a range of questions designed to highlight the emotional range and potential capability for remorse. These will be the first indicators of a possible personality disorder. The doctor will also need to study a patient's medical and personal history to establish if there is a pattern of psychopathic behaviour. It will also be necessary to speak to friends and family to get their opinion on the potential sufferer's history and compare stories with the ones you have heard from your patient.

If the doctor believes a personality disorder is the likely cause of the behaviour then they will refer you to a mental health professional who will conduct a further round of questioning and some tests. There intent will be to put your responses on a sliding scale and see what the final picture looks like. This will tell them if you have a personality disorder and, if so, which disorder is the most likely. Of course, a true psychopath may be able to charm even an experienced medical professional and may even be able to manipulate the results of any test to ensure it says what they want it to say.

There are other methods of diagnosing a psychopath and many are diagnosed after they have committed a crime and physicians have the opportunity to assess their behaviour.

Diagnosis of a personality disorder is only the first step; if you have managed to persuade someone to undergo the test and the results are positive then you will need to become aware of the treatment options and how difficult it may be to implement them successfully:

Medication

At present there is no known medicine to treat the psychopath. Science currently understands that the psychopath is a creation of genes and, to an extent a product of someone's upbringing. Whilst it may be possible to provide counselling for any trauma experienced during childhood; there is not yet sufficient knowledge regarding the brain and its make-up to correct any gene issue; which has potential caused a brain defect. More research is essential to understand the brain and any potential treatment options via medicine or surgery.

Medication is available for anxiety, depression and any other side effect which affects someone with a psychopathic personality. However, it is possible that these symptoms will not be displayed or that medication can be described for someone with these symptoms without being aware that they are a psychopath; hiding their true nature is one of the things that a psychopath excels at.

Counselling

Unfortunately, studies and research have so far indicated that the majority of psychopaths are beyond treatment. Their intelligence allows them to manipulate others and results; it also allows them to participate in group therapy and even individual therapy and learn more about the human make-up than they already do. As long ago as 1991 it was discovered that psychopaths who participated in group therapy actually had a higher chance of committing violent crime in the future than those who did not. Group therapy allows them to understand the best way to get under someone's skin and manipulate them into doing whatever they want!

The general consensus that psychopaths are untreatable has been held for such a long time that there is very little research completed now into treatment options.

However, it has been discovered that counselling is an option for young psychopaths! Juveniles who are still developing their personalities cannot actually be diagnosed as psychopaths even if they have psychotic tendencies. A diagnosis cannot be made until they reach adulthood. However, studies have been carried out using juveniles who have these tendencies and have been incarcerated.

The treatment is known as decompression therapy and must be carried out over an extended period of time. Instead of attempting to punish the bad behaviour that has been committed, the therapy focuses on rewarding the good behaviour. Every time someone who is receiving treatment does something good they are given a reward. This has been found to have a much better effect on sufferers as a psychopath responds to rewards and will behave in a certain way in order to get the reward they desire. They are extremely unlikely to respond to punishment as they have will blame someone else for the issue. Research has shown that, providing decompression therapy is carried out over a long period of time, there is a significant reduction in the number of violent incidents and repeat crimes which occur. The reduction in crime has actually been shown to save more money in future incarceration costs than it cost to provide the decompression therapy.

These trials have had less success on older people who are more inclined to seek their own rewards or look past the rewards that counsellors can offer and want more significant rewards. However, this does not mean that an adaption of this technique will not be successful in the future!

It must be noted that this is a treatment and not a cure; ideally this positive reinforcement will also be carried out by loved ones and family to continue the trend and aid long term stability in the life of the psychopath. Of course, there are many psychopaths who function within society's normal guidelines and have successful jobs and are pillars of the community. These are the most difficult ones to diagnose, but, if you were able to diagnose and study these people you would gain a huge understanding into the mind of the psychopath. It is even possible that a link would be highlighted and enable you to understand more about which treatment methods would assist this type of psychopath.

The Future

Research will continue into the psychopath, treatment options and what to be most aware of when dealing with them. The more psychopaths which are known about the easier it will be to assess treatment options and try new methods.

The majority of psychopath are intelligent and can learn to express the right emotion in certain occasions; even if they do not feel the emotion involved. This is known as cognitive empathy and is an intellectual concept. Emotional empathy is something that a psychopath is simply not able to feel.

However, research continues and there is speculation regarding the logic that the non-criminal psychopath is actually a benefit to society. They do not commit crimes and are dedicated to one line of work; often to being the best in their field. This dedication can result in them making a success of something which a non-psychopath would be simply unable to do. This type of reasoning is backed up by the case of neurosurgeon James Fallon who has the same faults in his brain as a psychopath but has never committed a crime and is dedicated to the field of neuroscience.

His research has been linked with Helen Mayberg's work; she has used deep brain stimulation to relieve depression. This was actually done by turning off a part of the brain and an instant result was found to be possible. Although this research focused on one specific point in the brain, the fault in a psychopath's brain is a much larger area. James Fallon has indicated that it may be possible to turn on one spot whilst turning off another and that this could have the desired effects; but there has been no testing carried out yet.

It has been hypothesized that a nurturing environment in the first five to ten years of life will make a huge difference to whether someone with psychotic tendencies develops into a full blown, violent psychopath or not! This theory actually supports the theory that children who are exposed to excessive violence will be de-sensitised to it and will think less of hurting others.

Understanding and Education

Perhaps the most important and effective way of treating psychopaths in the future is to educate people as to what a psychopath is and how they can be of benefit to society. If people are aware of how a psychopath develops and manipulate others they will be in a better position to handle them, or, if necessary, avoid them. Education will also allow people to understand that even a psychopath can feel loneliness and despair; they may often feel that they are looking through a window at the rest of the world; their only ability to interact may be through a violent act. Feeling so isolated can result in a conviction that they are superior to the rest of the world and that they have the right and privilege to do whatever they like. As their actions cut any connection to normal society they become free to commit more and more bizarre or violent acts. There are several cases of psychopaths who have killed simply to have companionship, it is almost unbelievable to think that someone can be that lonely when there are so many people on the planet, but there are many people who struggle to make social connections, some of which go to extreme methods to generate the company they desire.

Many of these symptoms can, potentially, be prevented from leading to a violent end result if people offer support and reward good behaviour. Even the most vicious psychopath is looking for someone to connect to, a meaning to their life. If people understood what it was that the psychopath needs there may be less violent crimes. Of course, education will assist in all walks of life. But, it is as difficult to educate the general public as it is to attempt decompression therapy on an adult psychopath. There is only so much that can be done with the current understanding of the disorder, but research and attempting new methods can offer a method of treatment. Even if only one percent of psychopaths responded to this technique, that is one percent less potentially dangerous psychopaths in the world.

It is important to remember that many psychopaths are not violent or criminal; even if they may have the capability to become violent. These are the ones which are living normal lives, using cognitive empathy to cover for a lack of emotional empathy. It is these people who are most likely to benefit from a better understanding and acceptance by the general community.

Conclusion

It is certainly true that a psychopath will feel superior to other people; they will constantly be looking to confirm this superiority by studying others, locating their weaknesses and exploiting them to confirm their superiority. In many ways this is simply an example of attack as a form of defence; the average psychopath lacks the ability to deal with an attack on their own character. If this is attempted they are likely to either change the subject and return the focus to your weaknesses, or, simply leave in a rage. You will be mentally marked by them and they will seek to humiliate you in the future by whatever means they can.

However, as with any disorder, there are various stages of the disorder. Those who are able to live relatively normal appearing lives and do not resort to crime will probably display most of the characteristics but have irregularities in only two of the critical sectors of their brain. Those who have violent tendencies are likely to display all the characteristics and have irregularities in all three sectors of their brain. To this extent it must be concluded that the psychopath is a product of nature and cannot be changed, or healed. However, if their issues stem from damage to just two sectors of the brain then it is possible that nurture has played a part in the development of a psychopath. This is a complex and extremely difficult area as there are too many variables to allow generalized results.

Psychiatrists are continuing to study psychopaths in the hope of learning more about how they develop and the best method of treatment. However, much of the research is carried out with inmates; these are, generally, the most violent group of psychopaths and have the least desire to learn. This is because the very characteristics which are seen as repulsive in normal people are actually seen as good in those within the criminal population. Working with the prison population may provide access to plenty of psychopaths which are less able to manipulate their environment. However, it also limits the effectiveness of any research as only one general type of psychopath is studied. As most psychopaths who have not indulged in criminal activity are unaware that they have the disorder, it is almost impossible to locate them and learn from them. The most likely reason for a psychopath to change is because they want to; when this is the case they can learn to improve their behaviour and integration. However, as psychopaths do not see themselves as having an illness it can be extremely difficult to provide them with an incentive to change.

Treatment via long term counselling is an option which has been tried and has had some success in juveniles with psychotic tendencies. It has also been successfully used on adult sufferers who have chosen to attempt treatment and have worked hard to integrate themselves into society. This provides some hope that treatment is a possibility; but is must be linked to an early detection and a willingness to change. The psychopathic disorder is one of the least understood disorders and yet an incredibly common condition. Perhaps most alarming is the fact that there are so many of them in the general population and that it is almost a certainty that you will be affected by one of them at some point during your life. This, alone, should be sufficient motivation to learn more about this disorder; its effects and treatment options. The more that is understood about any condition the less stigma is attached to it and the better the future prospects for all involved.

A psychopath feels no guilt or remorse for their actions, but it is possible that they understand on a purely intellectual level that their actions are wrong. If this is the case then it is logical to conclude that therapy and reasoning can make a difference to the way they view the world. Assuming they have the desire to try this then it will be essential to find a therapist which they can relate to and build a bond with. It is this which will push them into learning to control their actions and assessing a situation before acting. Instead of gaining satisfaction from manipulating others, a psychopath can learn to use their skills to help others understand complex issues and problems. They can gain the popularity and acceptance they crave by utilising their specific skill set to help others. In order to manipulate others they need to be able to see all the parts of any situation and then they will use your weaknesses to manipulate you. However, if their aim is to help you then this same skill set can be used to assess the options available and provide strategies and observations which can assist you in achieving your own goals. Being detached from emotions allows them to see the bigger picture and the most logical action which should be taken.

There is no doubt that the psychopath is a complicated individual, one that many people do not fully understand. However, this book should have helped you to understand what a psychopath is and how someone becomes one. It is a distinct and unique personality disorder that has the potential to do a great amount of good as well as harm. Understanding the types of personality disorder, how to recognise a psychopath and even learning the best ways of dealing with one, are all important skills to develop to ensure you do not fall under the spell of one. They can be experts at relationship fraud and mind games, but, in reality, many of them are simply looking for a connection to the real world.

This book has delved into the common misconceptions and the possibility of treating this disorder. It may be reassuring to many to know that there are positive signs regarding future prospects but that these require the cooperation of the sufferer and many years of dedicated therapy. It is not something which can be taken on lightly; just as the psychopath can dominate and manipulate your life; they can also learn to control their impulses and use their skills to improve your life and the lives of those around you, including their own in the process.

In reality, the book and even much of the research and therapy is simply scratching the surface. The human personality is a complex, evolving and constantly changing phenomena, there is still a lot to learn about all types of personalities; as well as the psychopath, but the first step has to be education. If everyone understands the needs and desires of a psychopath they will be better positioned to help integrate them into society and reduce the negative image and actions of the world around them.

Printed in Great Britain
by Amazon

71936190R00037